The Occasionist

Curt Anderson

Hip Pocket Press Mission Statement

It is our belief that the arts are the embodiment of the soul of a culture, that the promotion of writers and artists is essential if our current culture, with its emphasis on television and provocative outcomes, is to have a chance to develop that inner voice and ear that express and listen to beauty. Toward that end, Hip Pocket Press will continue to search out and discover poets and writers whose voices can give us a clearer understanding of ourselves and of the culture which defines us.

Other Books from Hip Pocket Press

You Notice the Body: Gail Rudd Entrekin (poetry)
Terrain: Dan Bellm, Molly Fisk, Forrest Hamer (poetry)
A Common Ancestor: Marilee Richards (poetry)
Sierra Songs & Descants: Poetry & Prose of the Sierra: Gail Rudd Entrekin, Ed.
Truth Be Told: Tom Farber (epigrams)
Songs for a Teenage Nomad: Kim Culbertson (Young Adult fiction)
Yuba Flows: Kirsten Casey, Gary Cooke, Cheryl Dumesnil, Judy Halebsky, Iven Lourie & Scott Young; Gail Rudd Entrekin, Ed. (poetry)
The More Difficult Beauty: Molly Fisk (poetry)
Ex Vivo (Out of the Living Body): Kirsten Casey (poetry)
Even That Indigo: John Smith (poetry)
The Berkeley Poets Cooperative: A History of the Times: Charles Entrekin, Ed. (essays)
Jester: Grace Marie Grafton (poetry)

Web Publications

Canary, a Literary Journal of the Environmental Crisis:
www.hippocketpress.org/canary.cfm
Sisyphus, Essays on Language, Culture & the Arts:
www.hippocketpress.org/sisyphus.cfm

The Occasionist

Curt Anderson

HPP
HIP POCKET PRESS

Orinda, California
2014

Published by Hip Pocket Press
5 Del Mar Court
Orinda, CA 94563
www.hippocketpress.org

This edition was produced for on-demand distribution by
lightningsource.com for Hip Pocket Press.

Typesetting: Wordsworth (wordsworthofmarin.com)
Cover art: Philip Rosenthal (philiprosenthalpaintings.com)
Cover design: Brook Design Group (brookdesign.com)
Author photo by Joe Gibbs Photography, San Francisco, CA.
See http://gibbsphoto.com/.

Printed in the United States of America.

ISBN: 0-917658-44-2
ISBN 13: 978-0-917658-44-0

For Julie

Acknowledgments

Poems from this volume have previously been published in *Poetry* ("Platonic Love"), *Poetry East* ("Hairstyles of the Gods"), *Bitter Oleander* ("The Ice Plant"), *Exquisite Corpse* ("The Auto Body Shop"), *Good Times* ("Riding Home," "Walking Home"), *Rag Mag* ("Good Morning America"), *Transfer* ("Litany," "Faith," "Poem"), *Barrow Street* ("The Licorice Suit"), and *The Porter Gulch Review* ("The Waiting Room"). The poem "Platonic Love" was anthologized in *The Poetry Anthology, 1912-2002: Ninety Years of America's Most Distinguished Verse Magazine* (2003).

I am indebted to my neighbor Philip Rosenthal for allowing me to use his extraordinary painting, *Flood*, on the cover. You can find more of his beautiful, witty, evocative work at http://philiprosenthalpaintings.com.

Contents

Good Morning America

The Labors of Love

Dark Room

The Golden Hour

Good Morning America

Good Morning America

may I direct your attention to the great orchards of ripening geometry
the diesel snores of the Canadians safe in the attic of our hemisphere
to the abandoned motel at the edge of sense surrounded by its moat of gravel?
there the venereal salesman lies beside the perennial blonde
her pink slipper drifting irretrievably toward fascism

on such a morning the birch shadows snare on the gleaming fences
the great rivers conduct their marriages in bookish silence
and the unfinished skyscrapers harden at the first touch of light
now shall we join the dough-faced immigrants as they begin
to sing our national anthem — but softly lest we wake the government

The Ice Plant

above the starry boulevard palms endure like mute rattles
black cars trickle down canyon roads to gashes of electric light
as her crowded cart chirps across a vacant lot and quiets at a curb

years ago she danced as the throb and prop of vacant men
pushing herself against the scratched glass of their eyes
until one day the glass shattered and blood spotted the bar

now those men slumber in the aroma of mint and aloe
their thick bodies floating on feathered mattresses
magazines open and gleaming like fresh trout on the floor

last night a black lab followed her back from the bakery
his cinnamon leash dragging behind him like a starved shadow
until she lingered at a bench to rest her feet and he was gone

soon the streets have sharpened from gray flannel to hammered steel
passing headlights project and erase her steps
she hides the cart in dusty oleander to climb an acre of ice plant

with day approaching and night ajar comes the hum of the hive
mesmerized passengers strumming by like dolls in pews
boarded and boxed as human freight embedded in speed

morning finds her stiff and blanketless on a bed of newspapers
hands vibrating to the waves of traffic passing overhead
her charred soles wrapped in the fleshy leaves — waiting for directions

Hairstyles of the Gods

the tease, golden
highlights, the wave,
the dye and bob,
the beehive, buzz
cut, the wedge,
parted in the middle,
on the side, slicked
back, cornrows and dread
locks, the permanent

Boredom

Rumor has it Boredom was abandoned
By his parents when he was small.
One morning a librarian discovered the baby
Sleeping happily in the overnight book return bin
Alongside a biography of Millard Fillmore.

As a boy Boredom constructed balsa wood
Models of famous Lutheran churches.
He dreamed of becoming a suave antiques dealer
Or perhaps a rugged submarine captain
Dozing at the bottom of the plush ocean.

Today Boredom is an unemployed teacher.
No one is quite sure of the subject.
To pay the bills he pulls a shift or two
As a security guard at the mall.
I saw him once wandering through Eddie Bauer.

Boredom lives in a condo near the golf course.
Sometimes you can spy him
Slouched at the window smoking a cigarette,
His brown polo shirt buttoned to the top,
A tilde of smoke above his bald head.

Boredom frequently stops by for meals,
Circling the table to straighten the forks.
He devours each course laid before him.
Even now, as I write this poem,
He is salting my words with dust.

Litany

let the night hoist its anchors
and the moon collect her messages
let the wind continue her manicures

let a lion leap from the jungle of uncertainty
let intellectuals be doused in ideas
let the hammer be smothered in echoes

let the oceans be musclebound and the fish finish pacing
let the rainwater rise and run away

let the song of color burst from the throat of the orchid
and the bees unzip the heat
let darkness be stacked in the woodpile

let the lips of the lovers visit their monuments
and their tongues break their tethers

let the ears not envy the eyes which envy the brain
which envies the genitals which are sleeping

let pain find his parents
let our feet be forgiven
let our blood run up the stairs of our bodies

let us take off our clothes like bandages
let us pray on each other

Self Portrait with Rake

Soon after we settle in the house,
I clear the yard to plant a garden,
Raking smashed plums and tangerines,
Severed geraniums, twigs and weeds,
Exposing a furry pit, a gray tennis ball,
Plastic shell from an Easter egg hunt.

At twelve I was my father's day laborer,
Plucking weeds and raking mown grass,
Tossing aside a walnut-colored baseball,
A warped Frisbee clutched by the ivy,
Or blood-dipped feather at the lawn's edge,
My friends jumping ramps next door.

Now there's a mystery to those years,
As if burrowing through time might unearth
Blackened keys, a bone-white lighter,
Rusted cap gun and matted feather,
GI Joe faceup on a mossy stone,
Ants crisscrossing his chest like bandoleers.

That boy's yard widens to a wilderness,
Straws of light poking through the canopy
To lost watches, wallets and clothes,
Unfinished poems spiked on branches,
A trail of lovers camped in the brush,
Scorched acres of death and divorce.

I bag the heaps and hoe the bald earth,
Mix in steer manure and scatter seeds.
Are we ghosts of our own discarded days
Drifting in the vicinity of what holds?
My jacket hangs from a rusty nail,
Frayed and bulging with deflated form.

Goldfish

a goldfish traces a circuit through four gallons of water,
brushing the spiked ferns with his copper belly,
then rising like a rusty fingertip to the electric surface,
to the shadow of broken light – what would the goldfish,
his lips pursed as if sucking a lozenge, say to us?

would he speak of his liquid globe stranded in a galaxy of air,
of rich silences interrupted by the mockery of bubbles,
of sailing over ceramic castles and mills, plastic gardens and wheels?
— and would our pale faces appear as waxing moons in blurry
firmament, rising in mystical regularity to bestow light and food?

the goldfish's entire life is locked within his glass sphere,
wrapped in the very currents he creates: his past,
present and future sharing those crystal borders — his color,
his joy, the very food he eats and the shit he shits floating there
before him, as the water grays and dreams of itself.

who among us could bear such self-containment?
all our actions floating about us — our purged words hanging
in air for all to hear, our movements sweeping back
at us in soft rebuke, the myopic sky staring mutely down
— after all this time, what would we say to the stars?

The Auto Body Shop

While I was removing your appendix, I noticed polyps and calcium
deposits in your colon, so I steam-cleaned it, and naturally I replaced
the clamp on your duodenum, and then I figured that while I was down
there I might as well align your testicles and sandblast the freckles off your
buttocks, and well, that got me thinking about the curvature of your spine,
so I removed and recalibrated each vertebra and replaced a few burnt-out
ganglia, not to mention the bushings above your pelvis. I also filed down
the contacts on your sciatic and femoral nerves. Your heart was idling a
little high, so I adjusted your valves, soaked your lungs in Gumout and
then welded your ribs back in place. Then I noticed that your lips were
chapped, so I replaced them with two rubber gaskets, which reminded me
to check inside your brain case, so I rewired your speech center, replaced
the universal joint in your brain stem and lubricated your hypothalamus,
which naturally required me to repack the bearings in your eardrums. After
I flushed out your memory, I discovered an abusive father figure blocking
access to nurturing archetypes, so while I was there I balanced your ego
and superego and replaced the cables leading to your libido. That's when
I discovered the burnt-out synapses in your logic center and this [hold up
a small algebraic equation] lodged in your anterior cerebellum. Finally, I
transfused your blood with adrenalized hemoglobin from a 19-year-old
track star. How would you like to pay?

Faith

I am tired of the angels
measuring my footsteps

they embarrass me
in their azure bowling shirts

I have waited at the end
of the runway long enough

my luggage is half sunk
in the concrete

lying on the beach
I am terrified

what if the waves
finally
break their leashes

who will save us?

The Licorice Suit

I admire the Italian wool suit and razor
       piping, your every question pushing open

the polished door of an unfinished
       building, where I point to portraits

of myself—the plucky pioneer, devoted
       first mate, captain of the debate team.

yes, no, yes, for 10 years skillfully
       filling a resume with marzipan.

sun's *an independent self-starter*, so am I,
       won't rest until I've eaten your family.

I'm looking for an opportunity to apply
       my panicking skills to your stately detachment.

each morning secretaries turn up the light on
       your dress shirt, a version of acetylene blue.

colleagues have admired my paperclip horses,
       surgical staples, my sullen parsed speech

dragged across the room like a clubfoot.
       I look forward to sleeping. my daydreaming skills

inhabit a small greenhouse at the root
       of my tongue. *my current position* is prone,

shaking your hand in the idle hope
       that money may fall out of it. *next steps*

include hurrying home to masturbate
        to the staff photos on your website.

I'm deeply impressed by your team approach,
        a scrum of lilac-scented MBA all-stars

roving down the hall and to the right,
        pausing, pinching the air for diamonds.

I live for this work, sir, for its ending.
        my past will send samples, references

a map to my current location. *thanks*
        for your time, so laundered and pressed.

if you need to reach me, I'll be singing
        in the elevator, filing myself in the folder of air

Drawing on Air

a pair of sparrows, sky and wire,
hammock sagging between two trees,
tending to the margin, her sweet shoveling,
lilies swing a soft oval, plates on stems,
mustard under the dorsal surface,
on a plum branch her straw hat, nodding,
tulips blooming against a slatted fence,
damp earth, mineral and chocolate musk,
leaves and gnats drawing on air

smear of chin reflected in shears,
lip and leaf off register, her humming,
a fence, a frame, husband and wife,
chimney and cloud, oak and air,
light blows off the high branches,
leaves swim to earth, to her determined crouch,
weeding around those lilies,
bees bumping the petals,
distant chainsaw shouting down a limb

sleepy husband folded over coffee,
butter and jam, kitchen window up,
sun a grain of corn inside a nest of fire,
hammers pounding horizon,
grasp and rasp of shovel, clock snipping,
damp floor of nettles and feathers,
rake submerged in grass,
she already planting bulbs,
shadow slung like a purse, lemon lovely hands

A Show of Hands

the hand
prehistoric

perched
on a knee

or sleeping
in the lap

I am writing
with the other

the one that empties
itself of ink

sews itself
back to sleep

how they move
through the dark like boats

cast the shadow
of the dog

wear the disguise
of the fist

how they dance
to the music of the tongue

world lover
beauty builder
ambassador

when did the thumb
like an angel
fall?

The Whiteboards of Ecstasy

Gentlemen and lady, a small detour has gathered our restlessness,
The drawn wires of slim resistance wander toward our shared desires.
Truly, are not the pen and the eye raised in similar manner? Shown
As an intermediary loosely clothed in possession, hanging in a closet
We open with drums. For these circles are vicinity, completion, a snake
Sampling its own length and feeling the end of itself, engorged.
So I start the outline of my own waterless crossing, a curve to boat
Back to the bow of her sweet lips, the white tablets of her eyes.

What rhetoric lulls and lifts off these scribbled skins, the gleam of a rear
Window reflecting off each monitor? In the sleep of language is the dream
World of love and its bloody soldiers. For a flowchart directs us to the town,
Just off frame, that is described in glaring affection, the village where our
Vessels dilate in praise of common attractions, or are erased by the waving
Hands of junior lovers, who disappear as we lie wrecked and smoking.
It is, after all, the form we speak through, the columns of chalk and color
Drawn over a plan of ourselves, a bed mounted as mission statement.

Before us the chemical mist of fraught letters and curled arrows pulse against
The possibility of agreement, consensus and flight. A candied-red underlining
The thread-black vision of prosperity dotted with rusty children, a hole
Between halves where love and memory wrestle our inborn projections. Amid
Charts and packets of sugar, our head pushes away and stands before the board,
Fluffing his calico tie, demos the dumb echoes of transport, the rhythm taken
Up by a nodding ring of tongues, until *anything else* is asked, labeled and addressed.
We are what we choose in an auction of unexpressed options, clock hands swiveling.

The Labors of Love

The Labors of Love

I would ride the great river of your hair
And lie stranded on the banks of your bed
I would ascend the stones of your spine
To sing in the chapel of your mouth
I would travel on the wheels of your song
And arrive in the company of a kiss
I would camp at the shores of your breath
To be carried by the current of your voice
My lips would sweep the theater of your face
And doze on the slope of your cheek
I would climb the stairs of your laughter
To study in the library of your eyes
I would map the constellations of your skin
From the soft observatory of your breast
My hand would scale your silky thigh
To sit sentry on the hill of your hip
I would kneel at the triptych of your sex
And copy this devotion with my tongue
I would lie awake on a long winter night
And be mother to a starving love

Platonic Love

We dine at Adorno and return to my Beauvoir.
She compliments me on my Bachelard pad.
I pop in a Santayana CD and Saussure back to the couch.
On my way, I pull out two fine Kristeva wine glasses.
I pour some Merleau-Ponty and return the Aristotle to Descartes.
After pausing an Unamuno, I wrap my arm around her Hegel.
Her hair smells of wild Lukacs and Labriola.
Our small talk expands to include Dewey, Moore and Kant.
I confess to her what's in my Eckhart. We Locke.
By this point, we're totally Blavatsky.
We stretch out on the Schopenhauer.
She slips out of her Lyotard and I fumble with my Levi-Strauss.
She unhooks her Buber and I pull off my Spinoza.
I run my finger along her Heraclitus as she fondles my Bacon.
She stops to ask me if I brought any Kierkegaard. I nod.
We Foucault.
She lights a cigarette and compares Foucault to Lacan.
I roll over and Derrida.

Midway Through Madrid

1.

hungry and out of cigarettes
I no longer attempt to speak

to the sleepless waiters who
ignore me with numb sophistication

but stroll by a stem of players
furiously plucking at guitars

the plaza swirling with blank
children behind parrot scarves

who give way to bronze gypsies
sipping the air as they dance

2.

calico skirts dilating and twirling
across four acres of stone

eyes plowing a lulling star
into threads of Talmudic light

I walk through an alley of broken terracotta
aroma of leather and sour milk

the music now a faint drizzle
falling onto the darkened rooftops

step over a detached chicken foot
embedded in the cobblestone

3.

returning from the city's dusty corners
I swim in the sea-green windows

skinny American with a scarlet pack
gun-gray sweatshirt tied around the waist

I imagine her face pressed to cool glass
six miles above the Atlantic

parcels of fertile land forming
roads and borders as she descends

I emerge near our little plaza
and idle in an empty café

opening my notebook to scribble a line
wondering when she'll land

In Golden Mist

in golden mist
I row to my face

water wrestles back
its chipped light

the way's been lost
for a thousand years

the mountain air
pinching an ear

I glide through
the darkened city

imagining soft grass
beneath my feet

the white cliff
of your house

I shift oars
in my lonely coat

Portrait

I have painted
a portrait of you
with my penis

it hangs lopsided
on the wall

my love for you
is apparent
in the broad strokes
of the neck and hair

your cheeks
are two red balloons
tied to the corners
of your mouth

which I am
still working on

The Bell

since you moved away
to a town none of us can pronounce,
we sit on twin couches awaiting your arrival.
O the long interstate of that.
you're never here to be
the reach of every word.
our stories pause at a passing car.
we watch the television tell us what we don't have,
waiting for the bell you have become.

or we open the door to darkness,
the folding moment in which you will not appear,
a slant of streetlight or hiss of rain.
we wonder why you refuse to wash away
the wreck of our chatter, the mixed nuts.
even the dour children hang on a twig
scratching the blackened window.
we hear footsteps on the gravel,
an old car door clucked shut.

but it is never you,
only the telephone rattling in the kitchen,
coffee grumbling in the background,
an explanation dragged out on a tray
with chalk-white cups,
our hands crumpling in our laps.
and now you are the silence we sit in,
the old stories appearing one by one,
threadbare and homeless.

Riding Home

riding home
drunk on wine and love
rain drumming
on the windshield
I think of the sadness of machines
of tears and their silk wheels

tonight
petals fall in my dreams
and float to your open ears
the old sorrows sleep in their boats
as though the wind had been dead
for a thousand years

Prelude to a Letter

I will discover where your heart lives

    I will put on the red face

        my mind will chew its way to you

         I will make sense of you

           build a country in the space you left me

            there is no happiness big enough to stop me

        I will unleash a forest of letters

        make a shrine of what never was

my better self being bedded there

I will petition for a hearing

          my little tyrant

      my

Dear Margaret,

I Was Madonna's Lab Partner

I was a disheveled English major, stapled at the shoulder,
She was the kind of woman who makes you want to streak a Psychic Fair.
Her hands were exquisite, two quartets conducted by thumbs.
Drums pounded inside me. I stepped towards her.
My penis hid behind my thigh.
She passed her smooth fingers through her golden hair.
There was a rustle of sonnets.
We made wild love on the gymnasium floor.
In the heat of passion, her augmented breast separated my shoulder.
And then she was gone.
I drank. My eye blackened behind a curtain of alcohol.
I lay on my back, a leaking boat drifting toward middle age.

Circles Round a Clearing

she rolls away, in the middle
of the night, ivory below

my tan arm. I draw fingers
along the trail of her spine;

her breath, sheathed in sleep,
a distant lamp pulsing in narcotic

darkness. then the morning
laughter of fishermen, as light

crosses the floor. she leaves
an earring perched on a silence

like a lullaby, dust waltzing,
returning to its rest almost lovingly.

sunlight jangles in the willows
across the lake, sparrows

sweep from tree to tree, as if
gliding from one mind to another.

Walking Home

walking home
drunk, trees
guarding the narrow
path. I shuffle
through the cold,
one foot listening
to the other. Her
cheek now lights
another man. I
hear only what is
behind me, fall
bled to winter
white, the wind
gathering its things

The Chauffeur of Desire

my love, I long to pull off your molecular sweater,
tender my cheek to the climate of your chest,
the garbled light of your breasts.

it is I stumbling toward you, towing the severed bed,
a crumpled poem in my lapel. I, the chauffeur of desire,
hunger in my hands, blind as a kiss.

The Master Race

I am married to the German barmaid with the clubfoot
I am always married to the German barmaid with the clubfoot.
We live in the penthouse of the Weltanschauung apartment building.
After dinner she meticulously washes and dries each dish
before hurling it in the air and skeet-shooting it with a pink shotgun.
I plug my ears and continue my expressionist painting of a clown
being crushed by an elephant.

She yanks off my clip-on penis and I drop my strudel.
I say, "Honey, I think we better talk about this."
Her eyes are two blue thumbtacks.
Das slurpin gewurt ein zeitgeist der slocken zist.
Although I haven't bothered to learn German yet, I instantly realize
that she is pregnant and that we are barreling toward a cliff in a rickety van.
I slam on the brakes and the van lurches to a stop,
its front wheels spinning bureaucratically over the precipice.

Gasping for breath I turn around to discover
a muscular Italian trapeze artist unbuttoning my wife's floral blouse.
As the beak of her breast nuzzles his moist palm
I knock him unconscious with a bound first edition
of Kant's *Critique of Pure Reason.*
He hangs limply in mid-air.
Splaten der uberbooster mederkamp vas slong meister.
A gleaming casserole dish glides past my head,
kicking up a trail of dandruff on my shoulder.

Fearing for my safety I politely jump off the cliff.
Shrubs roll past me like movie credits.
The ground approaches shyly.
I telephone the Little Death Mattress Company
and instruct them to deliver three king-size mattresses
to the spot where I expect to land.
Their polka-dot truck pulls away as I spot the mattresses
and change into my Jackson Pollock pajamas.
I wake up with the German barmaid with the clubfoot
I always wake up with the German barmaid with the clubfoot.

The Prettiest Poem in Town

a story of her elegant erosion,
the spoken sun, beauty bent,
slipping into a sheer pronoun.

a dab of ink behind each ear,
a necklace of pearly nouns,
and passion stirs in the proven

forms — as a den of readers,
detached, pleasant, addicted
to sound, recline as they please,

on sofa, caesura, a bed of letters,
singular as the camellia in her hair,
wilting into meaning, into this.

images bloom and scatter down
the page, its white mirror dangling
an iambic heart, rhythm slows

ending in a clasped couplet, in
the luster of voluptuous silence
— I am spoken for

Note to Self

No more poems about light
About the wilted petals of memory
No worship of ancestors
Or sacred solitudes pinned to the earth
No metaphysical diagrams drawn with a chalk moon
No pining for meadows of simple rhyme
Or beads of clarity on the silver window
No brazen manifestos to conquer the world
Or groveling before imaginary muses
No nothing

Dark Room

The Waiting Room

I hold for a sign of passage or release,
of light lifting off the abandoned face,
as though I had spirit eyes to see
the moment when death swallows.

instead I see arms and legs flailing,
tamed in turn and tucked under a blue sheet;
his breath thickening and rasping
as if to saw him into man and memory

when was he no longer among us?
was it in the tidal sheets where he fell unconscious,
one foot tangled in a beige blanket?
or in the ambulance as it lashed the houses red?

or when the doctor explained the declining electric pulse,
which measured each nub of thought,
bursting across the cobalt screen like a crack in time,
leveling to a single slumping thread?

was he lying down in the darkness of his mind
washed in one last wave of love or memory or regret?
or simply frozen in the moment of becoming
a spirit or a space?

for though his breath was the last soldier to leave,
though the errands of blood had nearly ended,
he hadn't put on the power of the unseen,
but lay conquered and complacent.

was his life a mere propulsion of dust
through days and years and decades?
or are his mineral memories
the very essence of my eyes?

when my time withers to ticks and whispers,
or fate severs this twisted rope of air,
when his courage cannot keep me,
how will I make a bed of an abyss?

Dark Room

for Robert C. Anderson

1.

father
you grow
old and human

the street tilts
toward evening

puddles blink
with rain

your head
drops

into my hands

2.

wicker chair and radio
his swollen foot caught in the newspapers

I turn down
the radio
pile the pillows

his rheumy eye
bends

voice
so close
it's inside me

"take my clothes
if they fit you"

3.

it is dangerous
to dance
with the dead

they look through you
like music

when they leave
everything
moves closer

the roses bow
the wreaths brown

the dead never stop
dying

4.

in the apartment
on McAllister Street

he turns down
the music

one speaker
working

he doesn't fix things

blows smoke
into the curtains

"you know they think
you don't love them"

elegant corrosive
silence

5.

once again I face the bloodslinger
room dims

the lights of the ambulance
sweep the street
red
blue orange
red

again and again
death spreads its legs

two beams of darkness

musk of dried blood and black earth
opening a hand
  a field

6.

we take turns
taking you
to the clinic

silver chemical
dripping
in your wrist

if you raise your hand
the flesh will burn

I can only think
to bring you water

7.

blessed be your birth
the regal walk and geological face

the mad operatic music
that wanders your house

blessed be your father
the Swedish sea captain

the shy Russian nurse
you married to your silence

blessed be your children
who are four fingers

8.

even when he went
under
the hands
would not sleep

gliding
from heart to head
and back again

detached

from the rest

until they sank

blued
at his side

9.

emergency room
white
hum of machines

legs and belly
buried in the blue
sheet

I comb his hair
back
take the hand

nurse says he must be
moved to another
room

we wait
outside

only the shoveling of his
breath

remains

10.

I tell you
the rain is ridiculous
the shuffling of night and day
the roaring roses
freshly minted spring
it comes to nothing

I tell you
the days are absurd
dust of light on the buttercups
the mechanical kiss of the heart
the doughy child
it comes to nothing

when I sleep I am buried in myself
when I wake I am raking the dark

11.

late night
impossible clock
can't sleep

where are you?

bed of clotted sheets
bed of bloody echoes

bed of the sinking
please

take your things
I don't need them

O the velocity
of your leaving

12.

gray cat sits on the grave
nuzzling its paw

the mind too
will lick this clean

grass heaves
where we stood

13.

I left you
in the chair sleeping

walked
to the water

turned to take in
the house

behind me boats
knocking

water kissing
itself

you lit a match
in the dark living room

your face
bloomed orange

went out

Elegy and Memory

no sleep since he painted her hair, photograph taped to the mirror, empty suit lying on the bed, boy downstairs sour, slamming doors

of her up to her heart in water, in a trough between watery mounds, feet lifting off the silky bottom, waving

once a chorus of whitecaps, now a shimmering surface, nothing to float in, just the smudge of shore, the sky's blue echo

what are thoughts, fanciful bubbles in the mud, bursting with the softness of spiders, she said, this time in a beach chair, straw hat blown off the planet

dawn breaks, night hidden in puddles and handbags, a comb of light across the bed, the banality of eyes, graves, memories lost in the bushes in the brain

why did he decide to paint her, from a photo he doesn't remember taking, something about the gray water, the waves of regret, the ocean of everything?

chance heaves birds into the sky, into minds, it's something like that, he muses, the empty dress of the mirror, the stone face

The Ineluctable Hearse of Memory

sprinkler raises its head to sing.
you grunt each dandelion

    out of that green. night climbs the fence
    crawls down from the trees.

        I no longer live in that house
        though it stands in my mind

    wrapped in light. aroma of persimmon and kumquat. smoke
    spilling on air.

you shoveling peat moss under the roses
up to your waist in darkness.

        now your body turns white as it leaves
        the blue sport coat fills with dust.

footsteps evaporate behind me, dog bark
shakes my blood, orange

    cat dips its paw in the bird bath, a lasso of flies
    descends on the roses.

the wind carries your grunts to the edge of the lawn,
then stillness. I am invisible in the tree

    as if surrounded by sleep. you are in the garage
    sweeping the dust off your shadow.

        the doctor says you are finished
        you are not finished. you are

there behind the magnificent
curtain of night. you are about to speak.

     even as your door slams
          on the pitching tulips
               on the deaf radio

                    on the sleeping water glass
                         on the darkened face
                              on the screeching planet

I remember that night cold.
the bed is always at the center

     of your death, its sheets streaked with blood,
     the clock staring across that plain,

a tap on the orange glass,
then silence like before a train.

     absence eats
         the house
            the robe
               the hairbrush
                  the photographs

when I was a child, we wrestled on your bed.
you in your night

     shirt. the pink quarter moons of the mattress
     swimming beneath the sheet, morning sunlight

tangled in the drapes, sound of a saw
breathing in the trees

Photosynthesis

I have a picture of you
leaning on a fence

your hand hovering
over the jagged field

leaves turning
your shoulder green

bird in the foreground
too close to sing

Drunk Found Dead Against a Backstop

shadow of
the backstop
on him
like a net

red wind-
breaker
tied around
his waist

lime bottle
empty
beside
inverted feet

glossy ant
trickling
down
his arm

head bare
and bent
toward
home plate

To My Heirs

take my things and heap them on the poor.
my notebooks and letters will fill a banker's box
to sit in an attic below photo albums and broken shoes.

for my ashes deposit me in a pewter urn.
lay my pound of dust on a bookshelf
to stand among the tomes of my fellow poets.

I will not speak to my reasons for self-slaughter
other than to admonish those who would speculate
on a fierce depression or broken love affair.

the truth is that since nature neglected to end me
I have taken arms against myself.
such is the fate of a poet empty of words.

as for my work, I gave all I had to my little poems,
though they now seem but poor orphans or worse.
perhaps one day my actions will draw a curious eye.

might an intrepid graduate student or fellow poet
shine new light on my modest verse
making a name of my scattered thoughts?

then might my end be a brave beginning?
the labors of the life earning a small legend.
the years parting to reveal wild-haired students

spreading my pages on wine-stained Persian rugs,
weaving my threads of ink into a tapestry of genius,
thinking me a Keats, a Rimbaud, a Crane

here he fathered a noble family of sonnets
forged in a collapsing star of love.
this the meter that gallops through the heart

carrying the standard for a new golden age.
and there the epic experiments which predict
the next fifty years of art and its cure.

no doubt with fame and glamour comes malice,
a fresh pack of academics to tear at my sleeve,
polishing each critical stone they throw.

or some bleak critic fresh from the carcass of a novelist
conjuring my purpose to embrace his obscure thesis,
my innocent poems forced to bear false witness.

by what right do these grand nitwits revise me?
collecting my scraps and collapsing my days
into a diorama of loneliness, failure and despair?

who will capture the essence of the man?
who will take ink to flesh out this abandoned life?
O, never mind, where's more paper? I'll do it myself.

Ghosts

One night my father appears beside me
His face the glassy white of church candles
"Why haven't you taken better care of my car?"
"Son, why haven't you refilled my prescriptions?"
Because I am poor, I say, and because you are dead.

Later my mother stands at the foot of my bed
Her golden face topped by a frosted wig
"Why don't you tell your wife that you love her?"
I'm sorry, I say. I will tell her tomorrow.
"And what's this about your father being dead?"

The Golden Hour

Poem

I was cleaning the house
when it went off

silence arrived
with a posse of memories

your voice was a wrench
that assembled me

there was poetry
everywhere

I Smell the Paperboy

2:10 A.M.

sleep departed without me
leaving a chorus of crickets
thrumming the bare attic light bulb
swinging from thought to thought
as a car rumbles by
leaves roll over on their sides
silence in the wake
summons the universe to a shabby bedroom
where a cat meows at the door
and tangerine musk whispers an image
through an open window
though that tree was cut down years ago

2:32 A.M.

left side of the world hums in the bones of the fridge
which rattles as if dreaming
of flight through jagged trees
a weary blackbird forbidden to land
on the dark branch that sings to it
and so turns to consider the right side of the world
where a slender figure
fills a tented fragrance
a coil of her hair
spent on a stripped pillow
the fringe of which flutters above the heating vent

3:03 A.M.

turning from expectation to expectation
of what doesn't arrive
of the silent partner stuck in mental traffic
or flung open in a broad pool of daylight
a ghost lying in a coffin of milk
my eyes slip beneath my thinking
the lunar ceiling a mirror in which I see
a billion errands overlay the pocked earth
a thread of sand descending
from an unlit bulb
a screen door clicks shut

3:12 A.M.

boss pops in jiggling his keys
a mole in a brown suit
the tropospheric comb-over
quivering sea anemone
would like to see our pudgy budget
would like us to think slightly outside the cliché
is sorry to announce the layoff…
is when my mind floats
in raw freedom and briny terror
as a time-traveling javelin
flies through the window
and pins him to a PowerPoint
of demons preparing his bath

3:49 A.M.

three metal taps
and the tides of the heating system
wash through
zebras cross behind the drapes
dry warmth bustles past the bed
pushing silence aside
my face floating to the ceiling
a dune behind each eye
and a thumb tack in each ear
I echo inside myself
the hum of the sun inside
coal-black hand crawls up the clock face
then down again to its cellar
for more darkness
for more time

4:01 A.M.

smirking boss
safe under a quilt of unconsciousness
the morning waiting like a carriage
to ease him to blundering success
the brown suit smarter than he is
I lick butterflies for luck
is what I should have said
but quietly packed up my desk
and rode the elevator
to a small country cabin in Grass Valley
where my poems went to live

4:22 A.M.

are there others in the universe
tick tick
I name the hours after imaginary friends
and pace the lawn listening to their speeches
no I am stroking the blanket's edge
the gate tapping out code
a car dragging a blurry beat down the street
tock tock
what's the use of waiting
a witness to one's own music
actors lining the avenues
hats over hands
the bells breaking off at dawn
thum thum
the heart pressing against the walls of its sleeplessness

5:36 A.M.

no letters to sleepers
dented faces on television
stranded shadows and loops of prerecorded information
that never arrive in our world
the man talking is asleep to the future
his head cushioned by a car commercial
a bomb in Israel
a celebrity arrest
the clock slain and gutted of its parts

its seconds
its minutes
burning like unseen galaxies
sound of blood circling an ear
wind through a bare tree

5:46 A.M.

sand filling the attic in waltz time
a tremor in the curtains
as the cat passes under
the waves of an ambulance
winnowing down Park Street
fear's finger pressed to a chest
a dog barks across town
faint aroma of fresh coffee and butter melting
or is it memory
like tidal light tilting
the edges of the eucalyptus leaves
the cardiac scrape and thud
of the morning newspaper on the driveway

Hiking Down to Stinson Beach

summer eyes sweep along
a western slope of stubble,

as steps relearn the broken path
branches climb to switchback.

the creek weaves in coiled volume,
lizards inching under our voices.

I slip headlong through the leaves
as sunlight splits direction,

brushing ferns and wild flowers,
erasing the doubt that follows.

leaning into a shady curve,
I float in a fiction of belonging.

the ridge gives way to open sea,
sandpaper shore torn at one edge;

lucid orange sky roughly ahead,
trailing a bale of copper wool.

across the headlands the bridge's spire,
taillights cloaked in pearl fog.

this driven home through the dark,
memory pushing the colors back

into dreams of hawks cutting the air;
alarm clock bleating beside us,

the topography of the olive bedspread
meeting the blue tea of the window.

Paso del Cedral

we descend to the tongue of the reef, to crayon coral,
sponge trumpets, angel fish disappearing as they turn.

ahead of me, her breath percolating, flocks of bubbles
rising sideways with a throb of beauty and retreat. she

about the business of seeing, even as fear and wonder
careen through me, a heavy rain bunching the surface.

she clears her mask and smiles, the raw radiance of that,
and points to an octopus jutting out, casting its silt

shadow. we're mannequins bumping the reef, our eyes
apart, flittering in the fishbowls of our masks, wanting.

even under water faint smell of hotel shampoo, Tabasco,
a crimp in my calf from the plane, ears swallowing air.

we wiggle through a cave, under a ledge a lone barracuda,
a lilting silver line with a jagged mouth, there and gone,

a displacement of attention, from form to emptiness to
the spout of her ponytail spread like ink on the water,

then a green eel, nurse shark, lobster the size of a tricycle,
spotted trunkfish. I glide over brain coral to a sheer cliff,

hovering, in a stream of time, pulled across, sound of parrot
fish nibbling the reef, cloud of French grunts receding.

a couple hours ago, napping, notebook open on my lap,
now under the ocean's skirt, a human bubble, a thought

drifting between death and air. we lose color as we descend
deeper, scraping our knees against the sandy bottom.

I pocket a pink stone and follow the others up, parting
the water with hands as white and hard as marble.

my bones hum as we wind to the surface, her fins before
me flying across the open water, lifting out of the current

to nets of light shifting around the boat's black iron. we
surface in warm air, throw ourselves over, unmask.

sun dipping into the hills, gathering rust. we sip beer
on the ride back, wind pushing color onto our cheeks.

the privilege of absorbing the water's message, carrying
it in the body to the shore, where it disappears inside us.

later we suck Popsicles, watch a cruise ship creeping off
to port, water worn around it like a white shawl,

waves spraying the cabanas, fringe of suits and towels
lifting off the hotel balconies. the sun's glow darkening,

singing in my skin. we stand at the rail, undiminished,
stone in my pocket, pebble of water rattling in my ear.

Blue Movie

lenses slide to swallow
fingers cocks and tongues

hovering like wasps
outside her flickering skin

light and angle conspire
to string love's crumpled holes

across the flattened landscape
of mattress and sheet

nomadic jazz mumbles
into the dead curtains

a treble clef of platinum hair
lifts off her cheek

as nipples gaze askance
draped in beads of static

swarming pixels gather
into a first tendered kiss

engines kick over and climb
groaning over each breast

for the jut and slump of seeing
spring approaching her thigh

each thrust throws its purpose
on to the staircase of another

with the curved discipline
of a sky polished by birds

sudden archipelago of pearl
at the belly's blurry latitude

lips curving around a vacant vowel
dimming to snow and hiss

The Golden Hour

an idea, rustling out of the woods,
short of time and film, I clank
around a stand of dim redwoods.

a host of large stones stop me,
behind them, a nation of boulder
and rock extending to the far hills.

the stones gray as gulls, gray
as waiting — clouds cradled between
shale hills and ridge, lit inside like tents.

tick of raindrop on my wrist, as sunlight
sweeps from stone to stone. here
I stand, a human mist on the air.

soup of cloud about the mountains,
darkening to drag its skirt of rain.
I drift slightly to the east — a spoke

of light igniting the middle ground,
burning acres in the mind. I still
to the lens, assume weight and position,

poised before the precipice of air —
a hunched figure, invisible to myself,
shadow cast down a copper gully.

lisp of wind in my ear, red-tailed hawk
dipping into view and gone, light
shifting, *click*, pausing, *click*, opening

Pushkin

Brocade and sash, the sword bound
To side with the chimes of her jewelry.
Darling hands, and then the dance.

Her neck a cliff on which an echo avails
A tucked fragrance, the necklace lifts
As pearls orbiting her breath. He

Admires the lilt of her mortality,
Window open on a shorn hedge, two
Persian ships and foppish sun; the

Music underlines a glide of seagulls,
Signals the light to enter a hallway unhinged,
Then sleeps in glib and feathery escrow.

At twenty paces the grave wakes and punts
Along the same estuary of grass as before, waits
At his feet, the pistol dangling like a pen.

The Properties of Joy

I salute the quilted strawberry
the yawning lamppost and dizzy feather

I bow to the gray bouquets of smoke
the wild banners of fire

I hook my ear to the strummed leaves
the symphonies of shattered grass

I sing the miscellany of desire
the porcelain lovers bathed in corrosive need

I raise my glass to the plates drenched in moonlight
the courtship of knife and fork

I take my hat off to the wind
which has already taken off its hat

I bow to the copper light thrown over the shoulders of the sofa
the clink of the invisible

I toast my shadow which is a torrent of silence
and salute the past though it is already saluting me

I wave to my own death
slumping toward me propelled by whispers

Holiday in the Sun

The wheel warms
As we snake up the Sierras

Car crammed with groceries and clothes
Magnetic Fields crooning in the background

It took three hours to stop
Talking about our jobs

June snow still lingers at the summit
Lifting its hem near the roadside

We pull over and smoke a joint
In the rest stop parking lot

I want this to be my life: filling my mind
with the music of chosen light

Let the vacation be epidemic
Let the bed be never ending

I'm ready to eat my weight in silence
I'm ready to star in my epic decay

Like Sinatra in the luxurious desert
Pulling his last breath from a wrinkled Pall Mall

I promise to sew my vague desires
To what is too beautiful to bear

Here's my hand and here's my word
They go together mostly

Curt Anderson's poems have appeared in *Poetry, Poetry East, Bitter Oleander, Exquisite Corpse, Good Times, Rag Mag, Transfer, Barrow Street,* and *The Porter Gulch Review.* The Poem "Platonic Love" was anthologized in *The Poetry Anthology, 1912-2002: Ninety Years of America's Most Distinguished Verse* (2003). Anderson holds a master's degree in creative writing from San Francisco State University. He currently lives near Santa Cruz, California, with his wife Julie.

CPSIA information can be obtained at www.ICGtesting.com
Printed in the USA
BVOW07s1805121114

374757BV00003B/148/P